Mindfulness Patterns
-A coloring book for adults-

Please enjoy these 50 pages of various patterns.

Our designer put all her love and care into creating these so you can feel more peaceful.

Pepper Lomax

Thank you so much for supporting our small coloring book business!

We are a small team of designers with a passion to bring the highest quality coloring books to you. We take a lot of time and care when designing each and every page we make, so we hope you love coloring these in as much as we loved creating them!

Your feedback is important

We are striving to create the best customer experience we can, so any feedback (good or bad) that you wish to leave, would be greatly appreciated.

Visit us at:
PepperLomax.com

Pepper Lomax

GET 35 FREE DIGITAL COLORING PAGES FROM US!

STEP 1: VISIT PEPPERLOMAX.COM

STEP 2: CLICK DOWNLOAD FREE BOOK

free download examples

Pepper Lomox

Made in United States
Troutdale, OR
08/09/2023